Animal Pranksters

Opossums

by Julie Murray

2

Dash!
LEVELED READERS
An Imprint of Abdo Zoom • abdobooks.com

Dash!
LEVELED READERS

Level 1 – Beginning
Short and simple sentences with familiar words or patterns for children who are beginning to understand how letters and sounds go together.

Level 2 – Emerging
Longer words and sentences with more complex language patterns for readers who are practicing common words and letter sounds.

Level 3 – Transitional
More developed language and vocabulary for readers who are becoming more independent.

THIS BOOK CONTAINS RECYCLED MATERIALS

abdobooks.com

Published by Abdo Zoom, a division of ABDO, PO Box 398166, Minneapolis, Minnesota 55439.
Copyright © 2023 by Abdo Consulting Group, Inc. International copyrights reserved in all countries.
No part of this book may be reproduced in any form without written permission from the publisher.
Dash!™ is a trademark and logo of Abdo Zoom.

Printed in the United States of America, North Mankato, Minnesota.
052022
092022

Photo Credits: Alamy, Getty Images, Minden Pictures, Science Source, Shutterstock,
Production Contributors: Kenny Abdo, Jennie Forsberg, Grace Hansen, John Hansen
Design Contributors: Candice Keimig, Neil Klinepier

Library of Congress Control Number: 2021950302

Publisher's Cataloging in Publication Data

Names: Murray, Julie, author.
Title: Opossums / by Julie Murray.
Description: Minneapolis, Minnesota : Abdo Zoom, 2023 | Series: Animal pranksters | Includes online
    resources and index.
Identifiers: ISBN 9781098228354 (lib. bdg.) | ISBN 9781644947623 (pbk.) | ISBN 9781098229191
    (ebook) | ISBN 9781098229610 (Read-to-Me ebook)
Subjects: LCSH: Opossums--Juvenile literature. | Marsupials--Juvenile literature. | Marsupials--Behavior--
    Juvenile literature. | Zoology--Juvenile literature.
Classification: DDC 599.2--dc23

Table of
Contents

Opossums

Opossums live in
North, Central, and
South America.

They live in forests and woodlands. They also live in cities and neighborhoods.

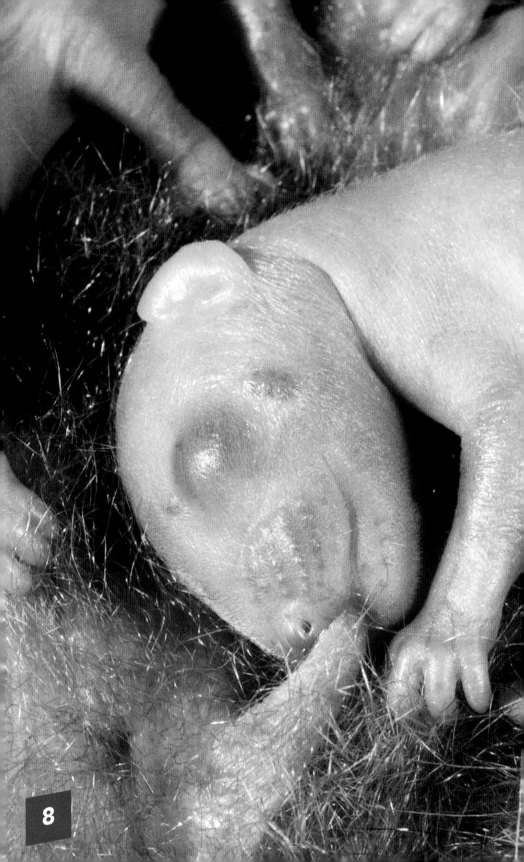

8

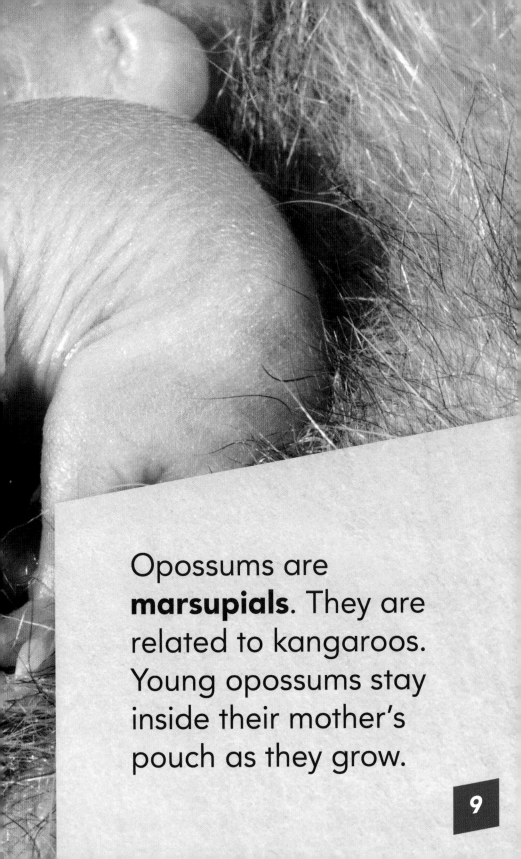

Opossums are **marsupials**. They are related to kangaroos. Young opossums stay inside their mother's pouch as they grow.

Opossums are gray or brown in color. They have round ears. Their noses and feet are pink. They have long, hairless tails.

Their tails can be used to hold onto trees. Their sharp claws help them climb and grasp branches too.

13

An opossum is the size of a small dog. It is about 2.5 feet (0.76 m) long. It can weigh 8 to 13 pounds (3.6-5.9 kg).

Opossums are not picky eaters. They eat eggs, fruit, insects, and small mammals. They will also dig through garbage cans.

Playing Dead

Opossums are pranksters. They trick **predators** into thinking they are dead. This prank is **involuntary**. It is a reaction to **stress**.

If an opossum is **stressed**, its body stiffens up. It may foam at the mouth and bare its teeth.

This is called "playing 'possum." It can last from a few minutes to a few hours.

More Facts

- The word *opossum* comes from the Algonquian word *apasum*, meaning "white animal."

- Opossums have 50 sharp teeth. They show their teeth to scare **predators** away.

- They are nocturnal animals. This means that they are most active at night.

Glossary

involuntary – not caused or decided by one's own choice or will.

marsupial – an animal in a group of mammals that includes kangaroos and opossums. A female has a pouch outside her belly where she carries her young.

predator – an animal that hunts other animals for food.

stress – a condition of strain or tension.

Index

Online Resources

Booklinks
NONFICTION NETWORK
FREE! ONLINE NONFICTION RESOURCES

To learn more about opossums, please visit **abdobooklinks.com** or scan this QR code. These links are routinely monitored and updated to provide the most current information available.